ARES &
ATHENA

A Philosophical update to
Sun Tzu, Niccolò Machiavelli and
Carl von Clausewitz on politics
and the conduct of war.

ARES &
ATHENA

Richard
Mollinger

CONTENTS

INTRODUCTION

The three most significant publications on politics and war are: Sun Tzu's *The Art of War (l. c. 500 BCE), Niccolò Machiavelli's The Prince (1513) and Carl von Clausewitz's On War (1832).* These publications have indeed aged well but current geopolitics in the West have morphed into something different to what could have been considered contextually in these books. This book was written to complement those works and reflect on how modern geopolitics requires some modification to strategic thinking.

In addition to the threat of nuclear and biological weapons, the early 21st century saw the Technological Revolution evolving under a body politic clueless as to how that revolution should or would develop. These political thinkers never had to consider the total annihilation of our species due to ideologies so toxic and reckless that humanity could blunder into such a disaster.

There are three factors in the politics of diplomacy and warfare:

1. Geography – resources, terrain, infrastructure, logistic flows

2. Climate – weather, suitable equipment, human physiology

3. Governance – leadership, morale and discipline, skilled labour and education

All three factors have radically changed since the initial publications of *The Art of War and The Prince*. The Industrial Revolution impacted them all. Carl von Clausewitz wrote *On War* in 1832 when the Industrial Revolution was only just reaching maturity. Therefore, the future geographical, climatic and governance mutations of the Industrial Revolution had not been considered.

CHAPTER 1

ARES' VENAL CONCUBINES

The Industrial Revolution was driven by laissez-faire capitalism, a system that demanded infinite growth, translating to an increased desire for the hegemony of empire. Infinite growth in a world of finite resources commenced an assault on the biosphere and led to fierce competition between states, ultimately resulting in war as a continuation of politics by other means. In this sense not much had changed except for the scale of slaughter made possible by industrialised warfare.

> *Rather than comparing war to art we could more accurately compare it to commerce, which is also a conflict of human interests and activities; and it is still closer to politics, which in turn may be considered as a kind of commerce on a larger scale.*
>
> *Carl von Clausewitz*

The sciences and engineering that made the Industrial Revolution possible were primarily used for exploitative purposes, commodifying all life and pushing the planet beyond carrying capacity. The laissez-faire introduction of the industrial revolution brought humanity to the brink of collapse in less than two hundred years. The Industrial Revolution massively disrupted the balance of nature. The pollution and destruction of entire eco-systems caused by the Industrial Revolution has ultimately resulted in climate change.

The first and second world wars extensively changed the traditional state political models. In the West a post-World War II economic model featured private enterprise subsuming empire. This mutation featured the military-industrial complex (MIC) amongst other equally abhorrent corporations. War was no longer about the survival of the state – it had become an extremely profitable venture, win, lose or draw. Multinational corporations pledged loyalty solely to financial profits.

In 1961, US President Dwight D. Eisenhower had warned his countrymen about the MIC. In private he referred to it as the military-industrial-congressional complex, referring to the government and its elected officials' interests in sustaining the MIC.

Initially, the US MIC had considerable operations in various states providing employment to US citizens, hence revenue. This would become a global model throughout the West. The MIC would thus generously donate to political campaigns and politicians that served its interest. The combination of jobs, revenue and campaign donations served as powerful motivators to support the MIC. The politicians who owned shares in these companies benefitted from dividends and increasing share value. The support given to the MIC included government grants, provided courtesy of the taxpayer, socialising debt.

The MIC model was then transposed to other types of corporations. Pharmaceutical, technological, financial institutions and others. They also used this blueprint for expansion. Government grants and loans were used to buy back shares, driving share prices higher. Higher share values provided bigger bonuses to executives and benefitted shareholders. These grants and loans were ultimately financed through taxation, privatising profits for company executives.

The prospect of domination of the nation's scholars by Federal employment, project allocations, and the power of money is ever present.

Dwight D Eisenhower

In the 20th century, under the cloak of democracy, the corporate state moved into politics, academia and the media gaining inordinate control of western societies across the globe. In the West, the state had been subordinated to serve capital.

Moving into democratic institutions was a matter of money and therefore relatively easy. Subverting democracy required control of the media, lobbying groups and donations to politicians and political parties. US President Ronald Reagan (1981–1989) was the first significant political figure in modern democracy that was schooled in the dramatic arts. It was to serve as a model for future leaders throughout the West where manipulative rhetoric was required in order to convince the public that absurdities are good ideas.

As of the late 20th century, corporations were able to move executives seamlessly between their own employ, political office, academia, strategic think tanks, non-government organisations, media units and government positions. This included elements of the military and intelligence services. Self-enrichment by rotating through political positions became normative.

US neoliberal/neoconservative (neocon) economic, social and political theories came to prominence in the 1990s. Neoconservatives and neoliberals consisted of a spectrum of convergent ideas. Radical Christianity presided in the neoconservative sphere whilst radical individualism belonged in the neoliberal sphere. Ironically the core of both elements was groupthink. That groupthink led to all sorts of self-justifications for criminality.

The neoconservative radical Christianity element had deeply penetrated the US government. Its belief in biblical prophecy led to close ties to US- and Israeli-based Zionists and lobbying groups such as the American Israel Public Affairs Committee (AIPAC).

Neoliberal radical individuality was atheist in concept but was supported by people of various religious backgrounds. Although neoliberalism was based in atheism, it displayed a poor understanding of the sciences. An arrogant core belief that they could improve nature and subjugate the laws of the natural universe to their will, existed in this clique. Neoliberals supported an emotion-based belief system often using pseudo-science, as if it were a definitive fact.

Science is defined as the systematic study of the structure and behaviour of the physical and natural world through observation, experimentation, and the testing of theories against the evidence obtained and is therefore eternally evolving. Science is the diametric opposite of ideology or emotion-based belief systems.

Neocon ideology provided significant support for the corporate state, strengthening the MIC and the security state with a resultant expansion of wars throughout the globe. It was desirous for a one-world government in order to better serve the corporate state. In this regard a plan to maintain US hegemony into the 21st century; the neoconservative Project for the New American Century (PNAC) was ideal.

The PNAC posited that the US was the indispensable nation and therefore US neocons were comprised of exceptional people. This ideology had been described as a narcissistic death cult; in a religious context it could be considered a war against God.

Neocon advocates rarely incurred any risk in the pursuit of their ideology. In the new paradigm, non-state actors aided and abetted by self-serving politicians had become instrumental in the creation and conduct of war without any risks or consequences, only financial gain.

All the war-propaganda, all the screaming and the lies and hatred, comes invariably from people who are not fighting.

George Orwell

In a clash of empires, the leadership could still feel a sense of loss, either in the form of treasure or family ties to combatants. The leaders of the Communist Revolutions in the 20th century took considerable risks and lost family members in war. Joseph Stalin and Mao Zedong both lost sons serving as soldiers in wartime.

What do we mean by the defeat of the enemy? Simply the destruction of his forces, whether by death, injury, or any other means – either completely or enough to make him stop fighting. The complete or partial destruction of the enemy must be regarded as the sole object of all engagements. Direct annihilation of the enemy's forces must always be the dominant consideration.

Carl von Clausewitz

What made this part of the Industrial Revolution particularly dangerous is that the centre of gravity as theorised by von Clausewitz shifted dramatically. The complete physical annihilation of an opposition army could not be considered the basis of victory. In order to compel the enemy to do your will, you must know who and what the real enemy is. You must annihilate the actual enemy and the ideology, not a hapless proxy.

A skilful strategist subdues the enemy without fighting and overthrows their empire in a battle of ideas. This is the method of defeating the enemy by stratagem.

CHAPTER 2

TARTARUS
DIGS DEEPER

The sparks of the French Revolution commenced in 1789, at the same time that the Industrial Revolution was gathering momentum. This revolution created ructions within neighbouring empires and sparked a series of wars. The outcome of this revolution was yet to be decided in the 20th century.

France was among the first countries to industrialise which led to the formation of significant clientele in many independent German states. The efficient industrialisation and logistical infrastructure of the Prussian and German states required unification which was accomplished between 1866 and 1871.

Federal Chancellor of the North German Confederation, Otto von Bismarck, was instrumental in the successful industrialisation of

Germany. This meant that Britain and France lost significant markets in the old German states. By 1890, Germany had become a dominant industrial power, surpassing France.

Oil was the lifeblood of the Industrial Revolution. The major shipping ports in the North German Confederation were Wilhelmshaven, Bremerhaven, Hamburg, Kiel, Danzig and Konigsberg. As all German ports were in the north, the shipping of oil from the Middle East was logistically inefficient.

A Berlin to Baghdad railway was proposed which had extremely significant logistical and economic advantages. A railway network connecting Berlin to the Persian Gulf, running throughout southeast Europe, was a threat to the financial empires of the British and the French. This railway would have accelerated the industrialisation of the Austro-Hungarian Empire and made Germany the pre-eminent industrial power.

The rivalries between Britain, France and Germany were about markets and resources representing a historical relationship between imperialism and capitalism. Power relations were about national interests, underpinned by corporate capitalism.

The First World War occurred because of an economic system requiring the Industrial Revolution to provide infinite expansion to maintain peace. Nation states came into conflict for capitalists' financial interests. The final bill included 40 million casualties including 22 million dead.

If my soldiers were to begin to think, not one of them would remain in the army.

Frederick the Great

The most obvious continuance of the French Revolution was the Bolshevik Revolution in November 1917. Imperial Russia had been decapitated. This presented a big problem to the victorious empires and was seen as a threat to the new masters of capitalism.

Empire and its acolytes that formed the elite were particularly outraged by the French and Bolshevik Revolutions. They found the savagery meted out to rich white people that constituted royalty, family, friends and acquaintances particularly appalling. These types of savageries were meted out to the poor and people of colour in the course of Empire on a daily basis.

And what physicians say about disease is applicable here: that at the beginning a disease is easy to cure but difficult to diagnose; but as time passes, not having been recognised or treated at the outset, it becomes easy to diagnose but difficult to cure. The same thing occurs in affairs of state; for by recognising from afar the diseases that are spreading in the state (which is a gift given only to the prudent ruler), they can be cured quickly; but when, not having been recognised, they are not recognised and are left to grow to the extent that everyone recognises them, there is no longer any cure.

Niccolò Machiavelli

The French Revolution and the Bolshevik Revolution commenced as reactions to the abusive power of elites. These elites had egregiously abused their power and were completely detached from the suffering imposed on the populace due to their ill-thought-out policies.

The industrial-scale slaughter of the First World War should have been enough to convince humanity that war should be relegated to the domain of museums. Even the bare minimum condition required for peace was not met; justice had not been delivered for the victims.

The victors were incapable of introspection or the consideration of their own criminality. The harsh conditions of the armistice imposed on Germany was the initial tinder to ignite round two.

You must know, then, that there are two methods of fighting, the one by law, the other by force: the first method is that of men, the second of beasts; but as the first method is often insufficient, one must have recourse to the second.

Niccolò Machiavelli

Peace in Europe did not last a year. In 1919, just after the First World War had ended, fourteen capitalist nations, including the US, Britain, France and Italy, sent large military forces to Russia to fight the Bolsheviks. The 'Cold War' fired up as a hot war and was still in play more than 100 years later, morphing into various forms.

In February 2024, the Munich Security Conference took place. It was attended by elite politicians from the US, UK, Europe and other countries. As these participants dined on lobster and drank Champagne they regaled each other with fanciful stories of their morality, goodness and exceptionality.

Avdiivka in Ukraine had just fallen, hundreds of thousands of people were already dead. In Gaza, tens of thousands of civilians were dead with a massive humanitarian crisis unfolding. Most European countries were entering deep recession and a third world war was looming on the horizon. All the ingredients that provided the tinder for previous revolutions were piling up in the West.

Princes and governments are far more dangerous than other elements within society.

Niccolò Machiavelli

An overwhelming number of Munich Security Conference attendees from the West had egregiously abused their power and were completely detached from the suffering imposed on the populace, due to their ill-thought-out policies.

CHAPTER 3

DEIMOS
COMETH

The birth of the Industrial Revolution was extremely significant in regards to colonialism. Colonialism initially reflected the Roman Empire where gold, spices and slaves were valued commodities. Superior military strength was used to impose colonial activities that were largely about establishing white-settler colonies and setting up trading posts and forts that supplied precious metals, slaves, and other products in demand.

Colonialism was an imperial theft of resources and labour using tools that included religious chauvinism, cultural genocide and violence. Violence included cases of extreme cruelty and actual genocide.

Slavery as a commercial enterprise during the height of colonialism was most profitable in warm climates for agrarian purposes. In colder climates the combination of the initial purchase of the slave, housing, feeding, heating, suitable clothing and training required to enable skilled labour for factory work were prohibitive. In places such as the North of the United States it was more cost effective to hire immigrant labour.

Western expansionism was made possible and driven by the disparity in technologies between the leading European nations and the rest of the world. The technical superiority of Western armaments, communications and transportation (railways and shipping) enabled the West to impose its will on their colonies. Minority rule by colonial masters required technical superiority, racism and the arrogance that one needs to feel exceptional.

The Industrial Revolution created a shift in the composition of goods in the colonies with a demand for raw materials such as cotton, coffee, cocoa, dyestuffs, jute, rubber, tea, meat, vegetable oils, wool and butter. The new markets resulted in radically modifying colonial practices that involved major disruptions of existing social systems extensively over the globe.

The East India Company (1600) was established to profit from the colonies set up by the British Empire. It was the first multinational corporation to militarise and try to slip the leash of empire in order to create its own independent private empire. British Government intervention became necessary in 1773 (Regulating Act), 1784 (India Act), 1813, 1834, 1857 until it finally ceased to exist as a legal entity in 1873. 21st century corporations became much harder to subdue.

US corporate interests and Wall Street bankers imposed their will on US foreign policy from the late 19th century onwards. US military actions in Central America, the Caribbean and South America (the Banana Wars) were carried out to impose US commercial interests in the region. The United Fruit Company was the prime driver of these actions due to significant financial stakes in bananas, tobacco, sugar cane, and other products in these regions. These military actions were suspended with President Franklin D. Roosevelt's Good Neighbour policy in 1933.

I helped purify Nicaragua for the international banking house of Brown Brothers in 1909–1912. I brought light to the Dominican Republic for American sugar interests in 1916. In China I helped to see to it that Standard Oil went its way unmolested.

Smedley Darlington Butler

Roosevelt's policies were relatively short-lived. In 1951, Guatemala saw its first democratic election in its history. The newly-elected President Jacobo Arbenz promptly extended political freedoms to all. Arbenz proposed the redistribution of undeveloped lands held by large property owners to landless farmers, constituting approximately 90 percent of the population who worked in a form of debt slavery.

The United Fruit Company engaged the services of the father of modern propaganda, Edward Bernays, to lodge a massive disinformation campaign against the Guatemalan government, accusing Arbenz of being a communist. The propaganda campaign and extensive lobbying led to President Eisenhower ordering the CIA to remove President Arbenz. After the overthrow Guatemala was ruled by a brutal repressive military dictatorship for some 40 years.

British Petroleum corporate interests aligning with US/UK geostrategic interests was again clearly visible in March 1951. The democratically-elected Iranian parliament, led by Mohammad Mosaddegh, passed a decree to nationalise the Anglo-Persian Oil Company based in Abadan. The oil revenues were to be spent on infrastructure, education, healthcare and social programs for the Iranian people. Mosaddegh was consequently overthrown by a US/UK instigated coup. Mosaddegh's government was replaced with a wasteful monarchy to serve as vassals and were supported by a repressive and brutal military.

The US, under the guise of fighting communism, was further involved in more than 36 regime change operations during the Cold War (up to 1991) with an increased frequency thereafter. Various guises such as the War on Terror were used. Grants to think tanks, non-governmental organisations (NGOs) and 'private' intelligence agencies acting in harmony with US policy were used extensively post-1991.

Empires have always been exploitative by their nature, expanding and seeking greater wealth and power. Its offspring capitalism superseded its parent and morphed into neoconservatism/neoliberalism, a chaotic system that erased the boundaries that traditional empires had. It had certain requirements in common with empire including military hegemony to continue with theft and plunder. The politics of empires were relatively more predictable and stable than the politics from the early 20th century onwards.

CHAPTER 3 · DEIMOS COMETH

In realpolitik, a perception of military strength and the capacity to use force underpins the total power dynamic. This effectively means that influence over others is wielded by control of information, which includes early indoctrination in the education system. Nazi Germany was a great example of how education and information were subverted as part of the power dynamic and were reflected in neocon ideology. Nazi ideology convinced the Germanic populations of Aryan supremacy.

The military technological superiority the West had enjoyed was lost early in the 21st century. The lack of comprehension of this change assisted the arrogance and racism to drive the colonial mindset to persist well into the 21st century. A fig leaf was required to deny that racism. Western-based media narratives were formed, underpinned by neocon economic, social and political theory.

The world has a way of undermining complex plans. This is particularly true in fast-moving environments. A fast-moving environment can evolve more quickly than a complex plan can be adapted to it. By the time you have adapted, the target has changed.

Carl von Clausewitz

The narrative was driven by the desires of a mutated empire and was designed to illicit emotional responses that served a corporate interest. Elements of that narrative had already been thoroughly interwoven into the education system. The problem with building narratives and propaganda is that the purveyors also come to believe their own falsehoods.

One of the great secrets of the day is to know how to take possession of popular prejudices and passions, in such a way as to introduce a confusion of principles which makes impossible all understanding between those who speak the same language and have the same interests.

Niccolò Machiavelli

As always bread and circuses are required to placate and control the populace. The daily news became part of the circus offering. If the populace is fed and entertained then no one will question what power is. If the bread diminishes, then the use of fear, a bogeyman and a proposed solution for that fear will keep the mob in line; that requires a narrative and control of the media. That media had been instrumental in shaping the narrative and building consensus in favour of wars and whose flag should be waved.

Four hostile newspapers are more to be feared than a thousand bayonets.

Napoleon Bonaparte

As of 2020, Trusted News Initiative (TNI), a UK-initiated media unit controlled overall information of the vast majority of global, including government news outlets. Its initial members included; ABC – Australia, SBS – Australia, NHK – Japan, AP, AFP; BBC UK, CBC/Radio-Canada, European Broadcasting Union (EBU), Facebook, *Financial Times, First Draft, Information Futures Lab, Google/ YouTube, The Hindu, The Nation Media Group, Microsoft, Reuters, Reuters Institute for the Study of Journalism, Twitter, Meta, Microsoft,*

Kompas – Indonesia, Dawn – Pakistan, Indian Express, NDTV – India, The Washington Post, with additional media units joining after 2020.

On an interconnected planet an ideologically-driven narrative controls a massive audience. It stymies the sciences, strangles debate and silences true intellectuals. It prevents great ideas from receiving exposure and realisation.

Men are so simple of mind, and so much dominated by their immediate needs, that a deceitful man will always find plenty who are ready to be deceived.

Niccolò Machiavelli

Even though elements of propaganda had taken firm root in Western societies, narrative control became increasingly difficult due to a very obvious hypocrisy. An unelected European Commission promoted wars, remained silent about the slaughter of civilians carried out by 'fellow travellers' and simultaneously lectured the world about morality and democracy.

The tight control of a narrative included strict censorship. The suppression included persecuting all individuals who exposed Western and in particular US government criminality. Journalists and whistle-blowers exposing state secrets including murder, torture, criminal conspiracies and subversion of democracy were hunted and imprisoned or killed.

During the second US led invasion of Iraq between 2003 and 2011, 150 journalists and 54 media support workers were killed. In Gaza, the Israeli Defence Forces (IDF) killed 77 journalists in 2023 alone. The Journalist Julian Assange was imprisoned for years in England's Belmarsh Prison whilst awaiting the results of an extradition request to the US on espionage charges. The US whistle-blower Edward Snowden was forced to seek asylum in the Russian Federation.

The legal system was subjugated by the body politic, which was in turn subordinate to the corporate state throughout the West. Prosecutorial abuse and failure of due process became institutionalised.

In the West, information suppression, control of massive propaganda and educational doctrines reduced the individual to servant of a global new world order. A tool to be exploited and reduced to an instrument for financial profit and ultimately war.

Those complicit in the waging of aggressive war had expanded on a scale not previously considered by strategic theorists. The MIC had been expanded to include the Intelligence, Media and Academic Complexes forming the MIIMAC. Academic doctrines had replaced scholarly and scientific works.

Narrations started to become absurd in order to manipulate consensus. The West bellowed that the world must follow 'A Rules-based International Order'; the rules of which were unknown and could be changed in the blink of an eye at the whims of the US government. On a planet that was well beyond carrying capacity, indoctrination and narrative-based propaganda were a slippery slope as they could only create a temporary diversion; they could not change reality.

A perfect example of this system was illustrated by the breakup of the former Yugoslavia from 1991 which resulted in wars between various ethnic groups that became particularly savage.

A NATO country as part of that alliance acted in the capacity as UN Peacekeepers in Bosnia and Herzegovina in 1995. The peacekeepers based in the vicinity of Srebrenica betrayed people under their care, surrendering them to Bosnian Serb troops in order to be massacred. It was an act of cowardice that would shape NATO doctrines.

The Serbian President Slobodan Milošević was vilified by the western media and political leaders in NATO states, accusing him of war crimes and genocide, including the massacre near Srebrenica in the 1992–95 Bosnian War. After the massacre near Srebrenica, NATO was seeking catharsis and the MIIMAC was keen to help.

Milošević was designated as the 'Butcher of the Balkans', a new Hitler responsible for genocide, particularly in the secessionist Yugoslav province of Kosovo. This was the justification for NATO's war on Serbia in 1999 that included an extensive 78-day bombing campaign. The attack on Serbia was based on fallacies that included the accusation of Serbians murdering over 200,000 ethnic Albanians.

During those 78 days the majority of bombs and missiles hit civilian targets, not military ones, killing hundreds of civilians in hospitals, schools, churches, television studios and even parks. The bombings completely destroyed Serbia's infrastructure. When it was over, international police teams descended on Kosovo to exhume the victims. They failed to find a single mass grave, there was no genocide. In Kosovo the final death count was 2,788. This included combatants on both sides and included Serbs and Roma murdered by the pro-NATO Kosovo Liberation Front.

Milošević was eventually taken into custody and placed on trial for complicity in war crimes that occurred in the former Yugoslavia. He was trialled in a court whose jurisdiction the US did not officially recognise. Milošević died of a heart attack in 2006, alone in his cell in The Hague. The International Criminal Tribunal for the former Yugoslavia in The Hague exonerated the late Serbian president, Slobodan Milošević.

The prosecutor of the International Criminal Tribunal for the Former Yugoslavia, Carla Del Ponte, revealed in 2008 that she had been pressured not to investigate NATO's crimes.

The modus operandi for justifying NATO's war on Serbia in 1999 was to become the template for other wars. The most obvious similarity was Operation Iraqi Freedom in 2003, carried out by the US's coalition of the willing, with a civilian death toll numbering in the hundreds of thousands. The justifications for this attack were even more ludicrous than those levelled against Serbia.

CHAPTER 4

EREBUS ENTERS

There are three primary colours – red, green and blue, but mixed they can produce more hues than can be imagined. Five cardinal tastes exist – sour, umami, salt, sweet and bitter but when fused they can yield more flavours that can be tasted in a lifetime. In Western music there are twelve notes, yet the combinations can give rise to more melodies than can ever be envisioned.

In political discourse an infantile binary understanding existed – right wing and left wing, Capitalist (democracy) and Communist (dictatorship) both of which are contradictory terms. A capitalist seeks to maximize profit by market dominance and is therefore autocratic. Communism could only ever exist with mutual consent. This binary discourse was deeply rooted in the Cold War (1947–1991) and formed the basis for controlling the individual through simplistic narratives.

The scale of war crimes committed during World War II by all sides had not yet been witnessed in the history of the world. The toll paid was the death of an estimated 75 million people. The most savage crimes were committed by Japan, Germany, the US and the UK. Between them, these four nations managed to kill over 50 million civilians by starvation, forced labour, gassing, massacres, human experimentation, bombing and immolation.

The US and UK brutality was mostly carried out by bombing and burning civilians alive. The British however stood out by brutalising its own subjects. The denial policy was a significant factor in the Bengal famine of 1943, starving several million people to death. Bengalis were subjects of the British Empire as part of British India. Instead of providing justice to the victims, show trials were held and a token number of Axis Power leaders were convicted of war crimes.

1. The main Axis powers were Germany, Italy and Japan but included Hungary, Romania, Bulgaria, Finland, Slovak Republic and Croatia.

Justice will not come to Athens until those who are not injured are as indignant as those who are injured.

Thucydides

Once, behaving like a beast is no longer necessary, the rule of law must be scrupulously applied to provide justice. A lasting peace can only be won by providing justice to the injured.

In order to claim victory and moral superiority, the US and the UK continued a discourse that was created for propaganda purposes during world wars I and II. This calculated and perverted explanation of history prevented the societal reformation required to enable peaceful co-existence. It was the failure to defeat fascist ideology espoused by the Nazi leadership and others in the West that made a peaceful way of living together (modus vivendi) impossible.

The aftermath of World War II saw countries trying to re-establish control over their colonies by force; using the same barbaric techniques they claimed to have fought against. These actions ended unsuccessfully as their colonies had now organised themselves and had gained access to advanced weaponry. Some campaigns provided pyrrhic victories which are in some ways worse than losing outright.

The Dutch tried to re-establish themselves in Indonesia in 1945, only to be defeated by 1949. At the Second World War's end, France tried to retake control in Vietnam culminating in a decisive defeat in the battle of Dien Bien Phu in 1954. The French, having learned nothing, went on to Madagascar in 1947, Algeria 1952, Cameroon 1955, Morocco 1957 and so on. The British were a whole different level altogether, involved in both Indonesia and Vietnam as well as the Greek Civil War in 1946, Somaliland 1945, the Malayan Emergency 1948, Egypt 1951, Kenya 1952, Oman 1954, Cyprus 1955, Egypt 1956 etc.

The socialist policies of President Franklin D. Roosevelt (1933–1945) combined with the industrialisation required by the Second World War gave rise to a prosperous middle-class and a somewhat de-stratified US society. The US had its greatest financial boom in the 1950s when the top rate of tax was 91%. The citizens of Western Europe, the major partner for the US in the Cold War, also benefitted greatly from this system, persevering with it for a longer period.

For a relatively short period; a little over 30 years, the bipolar world restrained capitalism in the West, with the exception of the MIC, due to the threat of overthrow by the communist system. The rest of the world was not so fortunate.

Since the inception of North Atlantic Treaty Organization (NATO)2 in 1949, up to 2024, its member states had collectively engaged in over a hundred wars. The US, UK and France were involved in considerably more than 30 military actions each, with some countries attacked two times or more. Even a minnow like Belgium had attacked over 10 countries.

2. In 2024 NATO consisted of: Albania, Belgium, Bulgaria, Canada, Croatia, Czech Republic, Denmark, Estonia, Finland, France, Germany, Greece, Hungary, Iceland, Italy, Latvia, Lithuania, Luxembourg, Montenegro, Netherlands, North Macedonia, Norway, Poland, Portugal, Romania, Slovakia, Slovenia, Spain, Sweden, Turkey, United Kingdom, United States.

Fool you once, shame on them, fool you twice, shame on you, fool you over three times and you are ready for natural selection.

Richard Mollinger

Collateral damage in neighbouring states, proxy wars, colour revolutions, covert regime change operations, political interference and neo-colonial coercion have not been considered. When these are added, the true scale of the death and destruction can be understood. The worst cases of collateral damage were the bombings of Cambodia and Laos during the US intervention in Vietnam. Not one of these interventions were due to an existential danger to the state.

These military adventures were carried out unilaterally, some collectively and others in turn. Vietnam was the best example of taking turns, with France the first to be defeated before the US and friends tried their luck and were also forced to capitulate. Together with the colonial wars from 1945 onwards, the ventures by these nations were rarely strategically successful in the long term; with most providing blowback of various kinds. The overall death toll was in the tens of millions.

Athens' biggest worry was the sheer recklessness of its own democratic government. A simple majority of the citizenry, urged on and incensed by clever demagogues, might capriciously send out military forces in unnecessary and exhausting adventures.

Thucydides

Considering that for the vast majority of these military adventures there was little defensible justification for war (casus belli) and no realistic end state could be elucidated, it must be deduced that political comprehension and diplomatic skills were woefully inadequate. It also takes an incredible arrogance to strategically lose so many military engagements and still cling to a sense of superiority.

Always assume incompetence before looking for conspiracy.

Niccolò Machiavelli

Sun Tzu, Niccolò Machiavelli and Carl von Clausewitz worked for, with and against skilled politicians and diplomats. It is doubtful that these theorists and practitioners could have conceived of the type of Western leadership incompetence displayed in the late 20th and early 21st centuries. War as an extension of politics means that it should only be used as a last resort when all other methods are exhausted.

Even though the Cold War was not considered over until 1991, the Union of Socialist Soviet Republics (USSR) was no longer considered as a serious ideological threat when it entered into a period of stagflation in the early 1980s. During this period, China under Deng Xiaoping's leadership was undergoing market reforms that embraced capitalism and closer relations with the US.

A minority of the population comprised mostly of the rich and influential wanted what they always want – more. The opportunity provided by the economic weakness of the USSR and market reforms in China led to UK and US economic and social reforms. In the UK this led to Thatcherism and in the US to Reaganomics; identical systems that privatised profit and socialised debt. The neocon ideology was born in this era.

UK Prime minister Margaret Thatcher (1979–1990) and US President Ronald Reagan (1981–1989) took the opportunity of USSR political weakness and China's reforms to destroy all semblances of real democracy, independent media and union power in their home countries. They castrated rules and regulations to free markets enabling legalised theft from the commons. A new rentier class was established through financial instruments.

In the USSR, President Mikhail Gorbachev held his hand out in friendship to the West. Instead of ushering an era of peace, the US actively destabilised the USSR and in 1991 assisted Boris Yeltsin to power and provided financial and other forms of assistance to keep him there.

After the collapse of the USSR in 1991, the West returned to absolute exploitation and colonialism through other means. These new colonial methods were reinforced with the US military increasing the number of its bases to over 750 throughout 80 countries in the world.

The USSR had broken up and formed several independent states. As the West had no direct corporate access to the bountiful lands in Ukraine and the newly established Russian Federation, local oligarchies were raised to assist in the ransacking of these countries.

In 1999 Vladimir Putin came to power, changing the course of the Russian Federation and effectively ending outside interference in the country. Ukraine was not so fortunate, dragging the Russian Federation into its vortex.

In 2014 the US was involved in a violent coup in Ukraine that led to civil war. The new Ukrainian government was twice militarily defeated by East Ukrainian forces from Donetsk and Luhansk who were being repressed by the new government and wanted regional autonomy. These defeats led to UN Security Council Resolutions 2166 (2014) and 2202 (2015), known as Minsk I and Minsk II. The Minsk

II agreement was underwritten by Germany and France.

From 2014, NATO member states assisted Ukraine in breaching the Minsk peace agreements, providing intelligence services and arming and training Ukraine for war against the Russian Federation. The neocons succeeded in turning brother against brother in order to loot the region. This was the tinder to ignite round three.

Of the 33 NATO states, 8 were formerly in the World War II Axis powers, 2 more collaborated directly with the Nazis and another 8 collaborated indirectly by supplying significant numbers of volunteer troops to the fascist Nazi Schutzstaffel (SS). Ukraine also supplied a significant number of troops to the SS and had its own fascist organisations who carried out ethnic cleansing.

When colonialism and racial segregation are also considered then all NATO forces had a recent history of extreme racial bigotry. Those handed-down predispositions were relatively easy to manipulate through a resurgent sense of exceptionalism against enemies as identified by the MIIMAC.

We cannot enter into alliances until we are acquainted with the designs of our partners.

Sun Tzu

War between the Russian Federation and Ukraine commenced in February 2022. This caused Ukraine to bankrupt itself in order to fight the war, paving the way for plundering of the country and sinking it into debt bondage.

Banks including the International Monetary Fund, against its own regulations, provided loans to Ukraine, yielding interest payments for decades to come. The US MIC's pockets were lined with money and their order books filled for years to come. The profiteering was not just limited to banks and weapons manufacturers.

Genetically modified (GM) and genetically modified organisms (GMO) foods were controversial. The science regarding health effects, environmental effects and wider implications such as monocultures was still unclear.

Up to 2014, Ukraine had banned GMO food but that changed after the coup. Cargill purchased a significant part of Ukraine's UkrLandFarming opening the country to GM and GMOs in agriculture. Through investment funds Vanguard, Blackrock and Blackstone; Dupont and Monsanto also acquired land in Ukraine.

As of May 2015, it was estimated that 2.2 million hectares of land in Ukraine were under the control of foreign-based corporations. In July 2021, Cargill became the major shareholder of Neptune, a port facility in Odessa, Ukraine.

In the wake of the 2014 coup, sons of influential US politicians were provided with high paying consultancies in Ukraine. Most of whom had no experience in the fields in which they were given portfolios and none could speak Ukrainian, Russian or read the Cyrillic alphabet. The most notable was the son of US President Joe Biden.

The first method for estimating the intelligence of a ruler is to look at the men he has around him.

Niccolò Machiavelli

Neocon ideology had completely divorced legality and morality, enabling legal manipulations and interpretations to facilitate some of the greatest moral crimes in human history.

For sovereign states, war was still a matter of life and death, a path to safety or ruin. War was therefore a subject of inquiry of which no details could be neglected but most did not adequately understand the machinations behind the wars of the early 21st century.

CHAPTER 5

A 21st CENTURY REVOLUTION IN MILITARY AFFAIRS

The collapse of the USSR provided a basis for Western and in particular US self-aggrandisement. A very much mistaken belief in Western military technological superiority coupled with the old colonial mindset provided the neocon order the confidence to attempt to establish global dominance. This dominance was to be supported by the US military and intelligence services and its allies as advocated by the Project for the New American Century (PNAC).

He who exercises no forethought but makes light of his opponents is sure to be captured by them.

Sun Tzu

From the early 1990s the US and various members of its NATO partners attacked numerous countries. These countries were all relatively poorly armed and equipped. The geostrategic control of energy was part of the reasoning behind these wars. Scores of civilians were killed and it sparked massive refugee crises. These attacks created no tangible end results, just mayhem and a mistaken reinforced belief in Western military technological superiority.

Western airpower theorists believed that the aerial assault with precision bombs and cruise missile strikes that had ensued as part of the First Gulf War in January 1991 was a revolution in military affairs (RMA). The actual effectiveness of the air campaign with the use of global positioning system (GPS) and remote sensing satellites was not that impressive. Overall, 120,000 sorties were flown with 84,000 tons of ordnance dropped, including 7,400 precision-guided munitions against what was essentially a defenceless country.

Within 6 weeks some 795,000 Coalition soldiers routed the Iraqi Army of several hundred thousand, incurring a loss of only 240 troops. This shaped US military doctrines believing full spectrum dominance warfare to be the latest RMA.

Blitzkrieg initially succeeded as an RMA because Germany's peers had not yet understood how to counter this new type of warfare. The technology that gave Rapid Dominance a greater lethality came too late for the Third Reich. That technology came in the form of the V2 and V3 rockets, the forerunners of Sputnik, intercontinental ballistic missiles (ICBM) and cruise missiles. The global positioning system (GPS) that guided cruise missiles used in the First Gulf War demonstrated the utility of unmanned guided weapons.

The Iraqi army was not a peer power – it had no credible air defence, was outgunned and equipped with outdated equipment. This action was a new technology version of Blitzkrieg warfare as refined by Nazi Germany during World War II. This pyrrhic victory led the West to pursue an outdated concept of warfare for the procurement of defence equipment.

The invasion of Iraq also demonstrated conclusively to anyone in the George W. Bush administration's crosshair the need to have nuclear weapons as a deterrent in order to prevent US invasion. This accelerated the North Korean plans for attaining intercontinental nuclear strike capabilities.

During the war in Afghanistan from 2001, there were indications that the US-fought ground war was not particularly successful. US military thinking was that their superior technological assets and firepower were instrumental in the defeat of Al Qaeda and the Taliban. Where fighting positions were prepared, heavy use of precision-guided munitions remained largely ineffective with the defenders still able to resist the invaders.

A major operation against the Tora Bora caves in the mountain ranges of the Safid Koh featured B-52 bomber aircraft and Afghan mercenaries to try and flush out the remainder of Al Qaeda. This operation was unsuccessful with many of the Al Qaeda combatants escaping to Pakistan.

Operation Anaconda in the Shah-I-Kot Valley in March 2002 ne-
cessitated significant reinforcement from 1700 British Commandos.
Intensive pre-battle reconnaissance had taken place, however less than
half of the Al Qaeda positions on a ten square kilometre position were
identified despite the use of satellites, thermal imaging, reconnaissance
drones, airborne radars and electronic listening devices.

No campaign plan survives first contact with the enemy.

Carl von Clausewitz

The Iraqi and Afghan insurgencies fought back with the use of
improvised explosive devices (IED), the Internet and mobile phones.
They used basic tactics that were much more akin to our ancestors, low
technology solutions for a high technology problem.

The heavy reliance on Command, Control, Communications,
Computers, Intelligence, Surveillance and Reconnaissance (C4ISR)
meant that specific battle-spaces were not well understood. Net-cen-
tric warfare needs fallback methods without reliance on connectivity
and independent action rather than a reliance on a centralised command and control centre directing battles.

In Afghanistan a coalition was built and other countries contributed to the cost of the war, but the brunt of the financial cost was
borne by the US taxpayer. The final capitulation by the West came
after 20 years of war but nothing was learned from this conflict.

The financial cost was not the reason for the humiliating capitulation in 2021. The US was already planning for another war in Ukraine just months away, which made military commitments in Afghanistan a liability. The capitulation freed up military assets, the most significant of which were Command, Control, Communications, Computers, Cyber Defence and Combat Systems and Intelligence, Surveillance and Reconnaissance (C6ISR).

The MIIMAC was salivating over the profits to be made in the impending Ukraine war. Massive profits were derived by the MIC, Wall Street and many other corporations from these military actions. As private enterprises were growing fat with profits, the West was laden with debt.

The Lockheed Martin F-35 became the main NATO multi-role combat jet and was sold extensively to Western countries and allies. It was the most expensive military venture in the history of the world, exceeding the financial cost of the Manhattan Project to build the first atomic bomb. The project had horrendous cost over-runs and produced the most expensive multi-role combat jet by far.

The F-35 compared to high end previous generation aircraft, was slow, lacked performance and combat range. The F-35 weapons' load was limited due to space in the internal bays and it was extremely maintenance intensive. Stealth features were no longer effective due to a new generation of radars and air defence missiles.

In the West the MIC produced weapons that were aimed at maximising profit not the defence of a nation. Hype and gimmicks rather than substance were the hallmark of the West's MIC. For nations that required a serious military deterrence, functional and affordable weapon systems were required.

The Russian company Uralvagonzavod is a prime example of producing weapons in a multi-functional organisation. The facilities were built during the Second World War to produce tanks. After the war, Uralvagonzavod tooled up to expand into agricultural tools, aerospace and construction. The production line is altered according to demand.

The T-14 tank as part of the Armata Project was the initial host of a family of vehicles with a similar base architecture. These vehicles shared a massive number of components and systems. The benefits include efficient production, logistics and future upgrades. It also provides for training efficiencies and the ability cross train soldiers to operate different categories. An Armata tank crew could be easily qualified on a Terminator (an armoured fighting vehicle) or other variants of the base model. As automation is maximized it would be relatively simple to upgrade these vehicles to be AI controlled.

Another example of cost-effective defence acquisition was China's dual purpose (military/civilian) shipbuilding sector. It was capable of constructing anything from large amphibious ships and super-tankers down to the Type 022 Houbei-class fast attack craft. The Type 022 Houbei-class could be deployed in wolf packs using swarming techniques. Wolf pack and swarming techniques would form the basis for next generation Unmanned Underwater Vehicle (UUV) and Unmanned Arial Vehicles (UAV) warfare.

The conduct of the US and NATO members were becoming increasingly arrogant. They became emboldened and that resulted in provocations and attacks on other global and regional powers. The US and its allies had become an existential threat to many sovereign states across the globe.

The US benefited greatly from Alfred Thayer Mahan's (1840–1914) theories of sea power in regards to US geostrategic positioning, expanding its oceanic strategic depth and requiring a substantive navy. The US relied extensively on a perception of geostrategic depth and its aircraft carrier fleets.

The US and other nations such as Japan and South Korea would regularly play war games in the South China Sea. In 1996, the US sailed two aircraft carrier battle groups through the Taiwan Strait to flex their muscles and provoke the Chinese. In 1999, the US bombed the Chinese Embassy in Belgrade, Serbia.

As part of the German unification, East Germany was admitted into NATO with the assurances provided to the Russian Federation that NATO would not move an inch closer to the Russian borders. As of 1999 that promise was broken, admitting 15 additional members. NATO further threatened to allow Georgia and Ukraine into the alliance bringing it to Russia's doorstep.

In 2002 the US unilaterally withdrew from the Anti-Ballistic Missile Treaty. In 2008 NATO made an agreement to place MIM-

104 Missile Interceptors in Poland, breaching the Treaty on Conventional Armed Forces in Europe (CFE).

Unfettered access to Crimea and the port of Sevastopol would have provided some ongoing relevance for the US carrier groups. Control of Crimea and the port of Sevastopol provides control of the Black Sea, its resources and its trade routes and was therefore a critical security concern for the Russian Federation.

On 16 March 2014, shortly after a US-backed coup had taken place in Kiev, a referendum to separate from Ukraine was held in Crimea. Four days later, Crimea became a federal subject of Russia. This action thwarted US ambitions to control Crimea.

The US interference in Iranian politics has been well documented since the 1953 coup. In 2018 the US withdrew from the Iranian nuclear agreement, known as the Joint Comprehensive Plan of Action (JCPOA). The US assassinated the Iranian Quds Force Commander Qasem Soleimani in 2020.

The Russian Federation, China and Iran developed weapon systems that made the US carrier groups redundant and considerably diminished the threat of NATO airpower. Naval surface fleet in-depth operations had been made redundant.

Actions have consequences. China, Iran and the Russian Federation each individually developed means of countering NATO power projection. The Russian Federation and Iran concentrated on systems that were primarily defensive. China's plan of defence was unique as it required power projection to secure resources; a large navy to serve as a type of extended coastguard formed part of that plan.

The next RMA was under development in China, Iran and the Russian Federation. All three had drawn conclusions from the West's bumbling military operations. Lasers, missiles, hypersonic missiles, layered air defences and drone technologies formed the basis of this RMA. An RMA can only be developed by an overriding strategic purpose that could not be provided by a profit-driven MIC.

Every age has its own kind of war, its own limiting conditions and its own peculiar preconceptions.

Carl von Clausewitz

The battleship had become obsolete before World War II. Aircraft carrier battle groups had also become redundant in the early 21st century. Layered air defence systems obliterated any notions of using air superiority to dominate a battlespace. The power projection of surface navies had been diminished and were reduced to coastal protection or to be used for operations against minnow states not yet equipped with tools of modern warfare. The very basis of colonial power had been neutered.

China, the home of Sun Tzu, developed the Assassin's Mace program. Assassin's Mace was the zenith of hybrid warfare encompassing political, informational, economic, legal and psychological, cyber and technological components in addition to kinetic warfare. Assassin's Mace at its full mode of engagement was designed to be total political and military war.

China projected a latent capability for the expansion of military power including an infrastructure that supported ease of logistic flows. This was underpinned by the power of wealth and a population that had the ability to ramp up production on scales not yet seen in history.

To defend itself against US and NATO strategy, China's RMA advocates including President, Jiang Zemin (1993–2003) recognised that it would be futile and prohibitively expensive to catch up to US military technology. New methods, technologies and a multi-faceted mode of attack, designated Assassin's Mace, was developed.

The cornerstones of the Assassin's Mace program included secrecy, deception and accurate intelligence on the enemy's most vital vulnerabilities. It was warfare as envisioned by Chinese strategists such as Sun Tzu, Sun Pin, Wu Ch'i and Shang Yang.

The governing Communist Party of China (CPC) and its People's Liberation Army (PLA) preferred human intelligence gathering (HUMINT) over C6ISR but utilised both.

Hence it is only the enlightened ruler and the wise general who will use the highest intelligence of the army for purposes of spying and thereby they achieve great results. Spies are a most important element in water, because on them depends an army's ability to move.

Sun Tzu

China's One Belt, One Road (BRI) was a massive infrastructure project across Africa, Eurasia and Latin America. The old Silk Road was also to be rebuilt through Afghanistan and Iran providing land access to the Middle East and Africa. The extension of the BRI was planned through Afghanistan, Iran, Iraq, Syria, Lebanon and ultimately into the African continent. Initially it had to be constructed north of Afghanistan due to the occupation of the country by US-led foreign forces.

The BRI was developed as an overarching strategy to develop a prosperous Chinese State. In time of war this initiative was required to keep 1.4 billion Chinese people fed.

In 2008 the Global Financial Crisis (GFC) was addressed very differently by the Chinese government compared to the West. In the West, the financial institutions largely responsible for the GFC were bailed out, further socialising debt. In China they invested in infrastructure, creating the world's most comprehensive high-speed rail system. This rail system reduced transportation costs significantly making it less expensive compared to shipping costs over similar distances.

The BRI is particularly important when considering the 'String of Pearls' as part of the grand strategy. This String extended from the Chinese mainland to Port Sudan. The sea lines run through maritime choke points, including the Strait of Malacca and the Strait of Hormuz. It provided strategic maritime centres in Pakistan, Sri Lanka, Bangladesh, the Maldives and Somalia. These bases also supported the Chinese Navy which was essentially an extensive coast-guard.

The naval base on Hainan Island was central command with the two most significant projects consisting of Chinese-controlled shipping centres in Hambantota, Sri Lanka and another deep-water port in Gwadar, Pakistan. The port at Gwadar connected to the Karakoram Highway, linking Western China and the Arabian Sea and also important strategically, situated some 300 kilometres from the Strait of Hormuz.

The Chinese government financed shipping facilities in Chittagong, Bangladesh and Kyaukpyu, Myanmar. Chinese state-owned companies constructed a railway link between Khartoum, Sudan, and Port Sudan. Chinese operations in Port Sudan were significant and they had agreed to build and finance a port in Bagamoyo, Tanzania. Primarily these commercial facilities were built for the expansion of trade but they were just like their shipbuilding capabilities and could be adapted for dual-purpose.

The civil unrest in Myanmar was an annoyance to China due to its investments in oil and gas pipelines that were at times attacked by pro-West forces opposed to the Myanmar government. These pipelines were critical infrastructure for the Chinese economy. The Chinese Navy would therefore provide the means to repel unfriendly states seeking to invade Myanmar or other strategic locations by sea.

Iran took a different approach to defence. Access denial formed a major part of the overall strategy in regards to possible attack by the US or its NATO allies. Access denial refers to an outright prevention of enemy access to materials, creating significant financial loss, loss of life and inflicting severe damage on the enemy, therefore slowing the operational tempo or forcing the enemy to operate outside of their desired range for effective tactical deployment.

Access denial to the Red Sea and the Persian Gulf was designed to inflict grievous economic wounds to the NATO powers whilst defending Iran's territorial integrity. Iran is a mountainous country with two expanses of lowlands. The Alborz Mountains to the north and the Zagros Mountains to the west create geostrategic barriers. These barriers also provide the ability to disperse military assets including command and control into well dug-in positions.

Iran since the early 1980s had used a combination of both soft and hard power to achieve greater influence in the Middle East. Iran, cognisant of their military limitations, demonstrated a preference for asymmetric force in the execution of their military strength. In the case of Iran power was defined as the capacity to influence the behaviour of other States and thus a course of future events.

Iran had been able to expand its influence and power throughout the Middle East significantly, through the use of proxies in wake of the US invasions of Iraq and Afghanistan, and attacks on Syria and Libya. Iran's main power is thus derived through regional political influence, global economic conditions, its geographical location and its resources.

Iran developed a massive missile and drone industry with military facilities dug in deep underground. The Iranian military engineered their own version of the Russian S-300 SAM as part of a layered air defence system enabling a solid defence of the airspace in the Persian Gulf.

Iran also developed wolf-pack tactics with large numbers of small, agile sea craft attacking targets from multiple directions. The lessons of effective wolf pack deployment had been learned and transferred to the application of UAVs, Thondar (Houdong) fast boats and UUVs to attack Gulf shipping and NATO or US fleets.

On April 1, 2024 the Iranian embassy in Damascus was attacked with Israel designated as the culprit. An attack on an embassy is considered an attack on sovereign soil. Iran retaliated for this strike on April 14 providing proof of concept for the Persian RMA.

After providing 72 hours' notice of an impending attack, Iran launched some 300 cheaply manufactured drones, cruise missiles and ballistic missiles in that order. The cost of the attack was in the tens of millions of dollars. The defence against these drones and missiles resulted in the downing of the majority of those launched at a cost of billions of dollars using Israeli, US, UK and French military assets. Assets that were in short supply and time consuming to produce.

The drones included intelligence gathering versions which mapped out air defence systems locations and responses. The majority of ballistic missiles employed struck the intended targets.

The Russian military possessed the world's most advanced hypersonic missile systems; including nuclear capable, electronic jamming, laser technologies and aircraft and rocket defence systems. All coupled with an extensive layered air defence system.

The Russian military demonstrated the capabilities of hypersonic glide vehicles (HGV) to perform evasive vertical and horizontal flight manoeuvres. The US had lost their geostrategic advantage that distance provided. The Russian R28 Sarmat with a purported range of 18,000 kilometres, at a speed of Mach 27 with a payload of up to 16 warheads, countermeasures and/or hypersonic glide vehicles. These missiles meant that countries like the US and all US bases, factories, command and control and logistic centres were in striking distance from Russian HGVs.

The Russian Federation was significantly advanced in ASAT laser technologies. The Peresvet system was purportedly capable of blinding surveillance satellites, with a megawatt laser fit for IL-76 aircraft capable of destroying low orbit satellites and disabling high orbit satellites.

The Russian Federation was able to easily outstrip the West in the production of weapons and munitions. Production capabilities were coupled with vast amounts of minerals, oils, gases, agriculture and other resources. Due to the cooperation between state and private enterprise in the defence sphere it was able to ramp up production in minimum time.

An RMA can only be confirmed by a series of battles. Drone warfare as part of the battlefield was instrumental in shaping a new RMA. The Russian Federation was the first nation since World War II capable of shaping this 21st century RMA due to the military action carried out in Ukraine.

CHAPTER 6

GEOGRAPHY & CLIMATE

Resources, terrain, infrastructure, ease of logistic flows

Anyone who speaks of strategy without understanding the basic building blocks of production, logistics and the supply chain is akin to an architect who has no understanding of mathematics, materials, measures and weights advising on how to build a city on quicksand.

Even if you understand the foundations of strategy, never assume that the ethnic and cultural limitations of production and endurance of your own populace can be applied to other ethnicities and cultures.

The bedrock of a state that is to be successful in prosecuting a desirable outcome in war is the comprehension of raw materials, production, terrain, infrastructure, logistics, science and engineering. A sovereign state must have the ability to significantly and independently ramp up production of war materials at short notice. That requires infrastructure, tooling and a skilled labour force.

The art of war teaches us to rely not on the likelihood of the enemy's coming, but on our own readiness to receive him; not on the chance of his not attacking, but rather on the fact that we have made our position unassailable.

Sun Tzu

Once the state identifies a clear existential threat to its existence then it needs to create a vast oversupply for the logistics chain. The draft of labour, capital and industry reduce costs considerably. Drafting industry, capital and labour is a cornerstone of total war, where all are required to contribute without exception. All minerals, oils and gases belong to the state.

This means growing the most suitable crops in regards to climatic conditions and principles of risk management. Storage silos must be provided to store rice, grain and wheat. Canneries are required for the preservation of fruits and vegetables.

To discover how much of our resources must be mobilised for war, we must first examine our political aim and that of the enemy. We must gauge the strength and situation of the opposite state. We must gauge the character and abilities of its government and people and do the same in regard to our own. Finally, we must evaluate the political sympathies of other states and the effect the war may have on them.

Carl von Clausewitz

During World War II, shortages of steel, oil and labour contributed significantly to the defeat of Nazi Germany, thus for the allies it was in production, logistics and supply where the war was finally won. The US had an abundance of raw materials at this time and was able to produce war material and supplies unhindered, which led to the ability to create a massive supply chain.

We are not fit to lead an army on the march unless we are familiar with the face of the country, its mountains and forests, its pitfalls and precipices, its marshes and swamps.

Sun Tzu

Germany required breathing space to ramp up production at home and needed to prevent the build-up of equipment and materials in Europe. German submarines were deployed in wolf-packs to sink merchant ships sailing in convoys to prevent the build-up of supplies destined for the UK and the USSR. The German use of submarines and sea mines in the Atlantic constituted a campaign of access denial.

If the enemy is to be coerced, you must put him in a situation that is even more unpleasant than the sacrifice you call on him to make. The hardships of the situation must not be merely transient – at least not in appearance. Otherwise, the enemy would not give in, but would wait for things to improve.

Carl von Clausewitz

The problem these submarines encountered was supply and, by March 1943, they were forced to abandon the Atlantic due to massive irreplaceable submarine and trained manpower losses. In simple terms, the Allies were able to produce anti-submarine warfare equipment for use in the Atlantic at a far higher rate than the Germans could build submarines and train crews.

Rapidity is the essence of war: take advantage of the enemy's unreadiness, make your way by unexpected routes, and attack unguarded spots.

Sun Tzu

On 1 September 1939 the German war machine was unleashed on Poland and 'Blitzkrieg' was born. Blitzkrieg proved to be an extremely successful component of German grand strategy. During the invasion of Holland, Belgium and France in May 1940 (operation Aufmarschanweisung No. 4, Fall Gelb) the rapidity of the panzer onslaught was tempered only by the supply chain.

Technology and over-engineering proved to be a weakness. General Erich von Manstein planned the Donetsk campaign for execution in early 1943. Hitler and the general staff believed there was a necessity for more panzers.

There are roads which must not be followed, armies which must not be attacked, towns which must not be besieged, positions which must not be contested, commands of the sovereign which must not be obeyed.

Sun Tzu

The required time to build, what was believed to be an adequate amount of Tiger and Panther tanks delayed the timing for the execution of Manstein's plans to July 1943, giving the Soviet Red Army time to construct a deep defensive line.

The Red Army at what became known as the Battle of Kursk defended with in-depth operations using an overwhelming number of anti-tank guns and tanks. For the Germans to successfully besiege fortified positions required a numerical advantage, they were instead outnumbered by a determined foe.

To achieve victory, we must mass our forces at the hub of all power & movement. The enemy's 'Centre of Gravity'.

Carl von Clausewitz

Skilled defence requires hiding assets. Surprise, manoeuvre and quantitative superiority awaited the German Army at Kursk. For anyone paying attention, Blitzkrieg had been rendered obsolete in a battle of peer nation-states.

The Soviet anti-tank guns and tanks were robust, simply designed and therefore easy to manufacture. The Soviets were able to vastly outstrip production of weapons compared to overengineered German counterparts. Vast numbers of simple and effectively designed units can therefore compensate for high quality.

In warfare, there are no constant conditions. He who can modify his tactics in relation to his opponent will succeed and win.

Sun Tzu

Post-World War II, the West followed the German example, concentrating on overly complicated weapons. Operation Paperclip saw more than 1,600 Nazi scientists come to the US for research and development in rockets, aviation and other weapons including biological and chemical weapons. The belief was that 'Wunderwaffen' (miracle weapons) to assist Blitzkrieg would be the key to success in warfare. In the West there was no comprehension that Blitzkrieg as an RMA had already been defeated.

Weather, suitable equipment, human physiology

Geographical considerations vary according to climatic conditions. Terrain that can support armoured divisions in summer may be completely unsuitable in autumn. The military and its supply chain are always at the mercy of the elements.

When operating in unfamiliar climates and geography you cannot attribute your own limitations to the indigenous people. If your troops have grown up in temperate climates then that physiology is not prepared for cases of extreme cold, high altitude, heat or humidity.

The French build up at Dien Bien Phu in 1953, believing the base to be invulnerable, demonstrates why indigenous limitations of production and endurance of your own populace, cannot be applied to other ethnicities on their home turf. General Võ Nguyên Giáp was aware of the difficulties of mounting an attack but understood the strategic importance of Dien Bien Phu. The garrison was vulnerable, hundreds of kilometres from Hanoi, the main source of supply, and it was in a basin surrounded by high elevations.

It would be a gargantuan effort for the Viet Minh to reach the mountaintops around Dien Bien Phu and position artillery there. By the start of 1954, Giáp had organised some 50,000 Viet Minh around Dien Bien Phu, supported by thousands of local peasants providing labour.

Tons of small arms, munitions and supplies were hauled up steep mountain gradients by hand. Artillery pieces were disassembled at the foot of the mountains and reassembled at the top. The local troops and labour force were physiologically adapted to the jungle, the heat, humidity and mountain slopes.

On the mountain tops the artillery was dug in and well concealed, then it was used with devastating effect. This action was instrumental in the capitulation of the French forces within 2 months.

Climate change has added a degree of unpredictability in both seasonal weather patterns and severe weather events. Luck is always an element in war but it can never be an element in military planning.

Therefore, just as water retains no constant shape, so in warfare there are no constant conditions.

Sun Tzu

When the Nazis launched Operation Barbarossa in June 1941 against the Soviet Union, Hitler had committed two grievous strategic errors. By attacking on the Eastern front, he opened a deep second front, which is something very undesirable in war. Overconfidence meant that a quick victory was expected, therefore no preparation for the vast expanses of Russia or the changing seasons were taken into account.

Deep mud in autumn slowed down the logistics chain, followed by freezing cold in winter, bringing the panzers to a halt due to the use of unsuitable lubricating oils for the climate. Hitler had not heeded the lesson of Napoleon's 1812 folly in Russia when the Russians used winter to great effect.

Country in which there are precipitous cliffs with torrents running between, deep natural hollows, confined places, tangled thickets, quagmires and crevasses, should be left with all possible speed and not approached.

Sun Tzu

Due to the various environments that modern armies may have to operate in, troops should be trained in various conditions for what provides 'game' fitness. The ability to march in moderate weather does not prepare the troops for combat in the mountains in Afghanistan, an Alaskan winter or the jungles of Myanmar.

Climate change means greater weather unpredictability. Therefore, a far greater depth of contingency planning, in regards to unexpected weather conditions and its geographical considerations is required.

CHAPTER 7

GOVERNANCE

Leadership, morale and discipline, skilled labour and education

War is the ultimate failure of government and must only ever be the path of last resort. War is the failure of diplomacy which is ultimately directed by the body politic.

If you cannot clearly elucidate why a war has to be fought, due to a clear existential threat to the state, then you have no casus belli. Without casus belli a war cannot be moral.

The consummate leader cultivates the moral law, and strictly adheres to method and discipline; thus, it is in his power to control success.

Sun Tzu

Just moral law is the basis of all legitimate authority. Laws that protect the very people that drive wars cannot be moral and should therefore be struck down. Only those who truly comprehend the evils of war can understand that it requires clinical violence that must adhere to all the rules of war.

No one starts a war, or rather, no one in his sense ought to do so, without first being clear in his mind what he intends to achieve by the war and how he intends to conduct it.

Carl von Clausewitz

War creates demands and urgencies that do not lend themselves to full bodied democratic debate. Some liberties shall need to be suspended and the body politic will need to govern in a more dictatorial manner. In these circumstances it is critical that the judiciary and media are fully functional and independent. In order for any war to be justified, any legal instruments must also be moral and adhere to the precepts of fraternity, equality and liberty in that order. A law that does not fit these criteria has no basis in justice and cannot hold legal weight.

The Russian 21st century RMA required the concept of air force, army, navy and civilian support to be obliterated and replaced by an integrated combined forces concept. All working for the common objective. Interoperability between disciplines is required for all military acquisitions and training exercises.

An army that is governed by emotion has no path to victory. Troop morale is critical, unless your troops have crystal clear, well-defined goals and are imbued with a sense of real purpose they will become unmotivated and lose focus, instead pursuing hobbies that include war crimes.

If your opponent is of choleric temper, seek to irritate him. Pretend to be weak, that he may grow arrogant.

Sun Tzu

Know your enemy, your allies and other interested parties. Know your own strengths and weaknesses. Education underpins all success in war and lifts the veil of blind hatred.

Grand strategy and its implementation need to be well understood by all those in high command. A victory is only possible if it has been meticulously planned before engaging in battle. There are theories that must be applied to all forms of conflict:

- All planning must account for an end-game that feeds into the grand strategy – objectives must be clearly defined.

- Understand the political and/or religious components of war.

- Understand the anthropological components of war.

- Maintain unity of effort with allies and build relations.

- Where possible integrate military logistics units with civilian logistics.

- Understand the limits of assassination of leadership as a military tool – what is under the surface? Understand the power dynamics.

- Understand the limits of military power – apply ruthlessly but only where absolutely necessary.

- High asset target destruction such as communication, electricity and surveillance sites need to be attacked with high accuracy weapons that limit destruction to the intended target.

Tactics is the art of using troops in battle; strategy is the art of using battles to win the war.

Carl von Clausewitz

- Aerial or artillery bombardment – consider aims carefully, do not destroy a target only to make it useful for other purposes (e.g. rubble for defensive shelters).

- In conquered territories use the police to uphold the law, this requires co-operation and relationship building.

There are five dangerous faults which may affect a general: (1) reckless-ness, which leads to destruction; (2) cowardice, which leads to capture; (3) a hasty temper, which can be provoked by insults; (4) a delicacy of honour which is sensitive to shame; (5) over-solicitude for his men, which exposes him to worry and trouble.

Sun Tzu

- At an operational level, goals and objectives must be clearly defined and succinctly explained to the commanders and troops executing the mission. Common sense is not as common as you think, so when giving orders check for comprehension.

- No orders should prevent initiative. At times only commanders at the frontline can see opportunities that present themselves. They must be allowed to take the advantage and achieve greater objectives than those defined.

The captured soldiers should be kindly treated and kept.

Sun Tzu

- In combat act without passion and/or hate. Respect defeated enemies.

- Uphold the highest standards of moral and ethical conduct – officers and NCOs must be moral exemplars.

- Trusted and competent language specialists are crucial for operations – Competency requires suitable body language training in addition to knowledge of language nuances.

The wars in Afghanistan (October 2001) and Iraq (March 2003) started as conventional conflicts. The first problem that occurs when invading any country, regardless of motivation, is that you are the invader. Unless loss of life incurred by the country invaded is modest and people's lives are considerably better off post invasion, in a relatively short period of time, there will be dissent and insurrection against the occupying power(s).

The reasons for the George W. Bush administration losing legitimacy for the War on Terror and support for their neocon agenda is a long list. Events such as the invasion of Iraq and the torture facilities in Guantanamo Bay, Abu Ghraib and other places were at the forefront.

Discipline must be rigidly enforced and crimes prosecuted from the top down. All who participate in war crimes whether by act of deliberate omission or direct participation must be prosecuted and punished. Murder, torture and rape not only destroy the legitimacy of using force it also undermines both discipline and morale like a cancerous growth.

Therefore, soldiers must be treated in the first instance with humanity, but kept under control by means of iron discipline. This is a certain road to victory.

Sun Tzu

Criminals and mercenaries are attracted to insurgencies therefore order must be restored immediately. To prevent insurgencies there are about 30 peacekeepers (comprised of military police, civilian police and/or soldiers) required per 1,000 head of population. Control of information is critical at this juncture. War criminals must be brought to justice as quickly as possible and trials conducted with all due fairness and transparency.

Grand strategy demands that justice, security, good governance, essential services and economic development are supplied to all. Reconstruction, employment and education are the building blocks necessary for the rebuilding of any society in order to provide a peace. These basic requirements were neglected in the aftermaths of the invasions of both Afghanistan and Iraq, allowing discontent to fester among the population.

Effective leadership is forged in childhood, the period when creativity, emotional intelligence, empathy and moral courage develop. They resist cultural indoctrination. Cultural indoctrination provides a perspective through which we see issues.

The state that separates its scholars from its warriors will have its thinking done by cowards, and its fighting done by fools.

Thucydides

Leadership qualities are tempered in adulthood by hard lessons and failures that test integrity and provide humility. A leader listens and checks for facts and detail. A leader shares credit but is always fully accountable for all actions. Most of all a leader serves others.

Two qualities are indispensable: first, an intellect that, even in the darkest hour, retains some glimmerings of the inner light which leads to truth; and second, the courage to follow this faint light wherever it may lead.

Carl von Clausewitz

Leaders must be selected only by merit. Napoleon's Grande Armée owed much of its success to the marshals appointed by Napoleon. Meritocracy creates great commanders. Historical exemplary military leaders include:

- Themistocles
- Alexander the Great
- Julius Caesar
- Salah ad-Din Yusuf ibn Ayyub (Saladin)
- Friedrich II (Frederick the Great) House of Hohenzollern
- Giuseppe Garibaldi
- Helmuth von Moltke
- Horatio Nelson
- John Monash
- Mustafa Kemal Ataturk
- Smedley Darlington Butler
- George C. Marshall
- Isoroku Yamamoto
- Georgy Zhukov
- Erwin Rommel
- Võ Nguyên Giáp
- Fidel Castro

Leadership selection is most important at an operational level. An intelligent, agile mind and courage are required at all leadership levels. It is equally important for officers to have both physical and moral courage. Officers without moral courage are not suitable for commissioned wartime service.

Strength of character does not consist solely in having powerful feelings, but in maintaining one's balance in spite of them. Even with the violence of emotion, judgment and principle must still function like a ship's compass, which records the slightest variations however rough the sea.

Carl von Clausewitz

All soldiers and civil counterparts necessary for the prosecution of war are brothers in arms regardless of sex, nationality, sexuality, race or religion. All must act with dignified and modest behaviour.

CHAPTER 8

GRAND STRATEGY REVISED

The motivators for the French Revolution being fraternity, equality and liberty must be the driving force for 'just war'. All planning in regards to warfare must ultimately be about establishing a lasting peace.

Justice for all can be the only precept for casus belli. The principle of just war therefore lays either in self-defence or in defending against deliberate acts of crimes against humanity, barbarism and/or violent aggression to a particular culture or group.

If war has to be fought then it must act as an engine of change for the betterment of mankind. The outcome of successful wars can only be measured in terms of diminishing conflicts over time, until it ceases to exist as a human activity.

Savage peoples are ruled by passion, civilized peoples by the mind.

Carl von Clausewitz

To command a global battle-space or a regional battle-space means controlling space, sub-aquatic space and cyber-space, or at least controlling space, sub-aquatic space and your own cyber-space.

Even though weapons selections are made at a philosophical and at the grand strategic level their deployment takes place at the operational level. Strategic nuclear weapons are only useful as a deterrence, when unleashed they constitute a crime against humanity. Chemical, biological and gene editing weapons constitute crimes against humanity and have no place in warfare.

The use of petroleum-based incendiaries such as napalm and other overtly cruel weapons such as white phosphorous must be banned. Nuclear-tipped bunker buster bombs cause widespread damage and leave lasting radiation contamination. Once a nuclear weapon is used, an escalation ladder can quickly result in a full nuclear exchange.

Where large-scale destruction is required thermobaric weapons (vacuum bombs) are far more appropriate, as they are now compatible in destructive capability with atomic weapons but they do not leave long-term effects on the environment. The use of thermobaric weapons still needs to be limited to legitimate targets.

Destruction of military targets is a pointless exercise if it does not result in imposing your will on the enemy. Neocon ideology and the PNAC drove nearly all wars post 1991. Theft through the use of violence was the modus operandi but a modus vivendi was never considered. You cannot impose your will unless there is a plan of how you will coexist in the aftermath; the war will simply mutate and continue.

From a neocon perspective, living on a planet that was well past carrying capacity, a hegemonic PNAC required unfettered access to all resources. The project could not come to fruition without the bountiful lands of Belarus, Ukraine and Russia. Given the economic model of the time, the neocons would have descended on these lands like a plague of locusts.

Strategy could be described as a game of poker. A good analogy for NATO was a gambler who is losing and continuously doubles down in order to recover the losses. As such, NATO's final gamble was a bluff against an opponent holding four aces in a one pack game. NATO states were playing on house credit ultimately bankrolled by the taxpayer.

The 2014 coup in Ukraine resulted in changes to the law mandated by the new US-backed government. Some of these laws were contrary to the United Nations Declaration of Human Rights and were directed at the Russian-speaking communities. This led to outrage in the Russian-speaking communities and was further antagonised by a fierce repression against these areas. The repressions carried out in Odessa and Mariupol were particularly brutal. In Odessa, civilians were burned alive.

As a result of the oppression of the Russian-speaking community Donetsk and Luhansk provinces voted for a status of autonomy. Russian-speaking Ukrainian military units went over to the autonomist side in these areas, successfully defending the region from the Ukrainian army. Forcing the Ukrainian government to commit to the Minsk agreements providing guarantees to the autonomists.

All warfare is based on deception.

Sun Tzu

Just a few months after signing the agreement, the new Ukrainian president, Poroshenko, launched a massive operation against the Donbas advised by NATO officers. In early 2015, the Ukrainian national forces were encircled by the Ukrainian autonomists and decisively defeated at Debaltsevo, which was turning into a bloodbath.

German Chancellor Angela Merkel flew to Moscow to ask Russian President Vladimir Putin to intercede and mitigate the violence. The Minsk II agreements were signed shortly thereafter with Germany and France as guarantors.

Interceding in the Ukrainian Civil War was a grave error on the part of the Russian Federation. Mercy can only be provided to honourable people. Deliberately breaching the Minsk I agreements was a clear indication that those involved had no integrity.

After the defeat in 2015, due to a lack of soldiers, the Ukrainian government used paramilitary units composed of far right-wing militants and foreign mercenaries. These far-right militants were trained by the US, UK, Canada and France. The purpose of these troops was to continue harassing the Donetsk and Luhansk territories and ultimately to take Crimea and attack the Russian Federation. The US vassal Ukrainian government and NATO had no intention of adhering to either the Minsk I or II agreements.

Kind-hearted people might of course think there was some ingenious way to disarm or defeat an enemy without too much bloodshed, and might imagine this is the true goal of the art of war. Pleasant as it sounds; it is a fallacy that must be exposed: War is such a dangerous business that the mistakes which come from kindness are the very worst.

Carl von Clausewitz

Permitting the slaughter of the troops in the cauldron until capitulation would have been the end of the imposed Ukrainian government, changing the political dynamics in the region. Allowing the Ukrainian government to recover, and with the help of NATO countries, re-constitute a massive army resulted in combat mortality rates not seen since the two world wars.

The PNAC never provided for a modus vivendi. The defeat of neocon ideology and the PNAC was possible at Debaltsevo, and its aftermath, had the issue been dealt with decisively at that point and followed up with global strategic economic reforms.

People should either be caressed or crushed. If you do them minor damage they will get their revenge; but if you cripple them there is nothing they can do. If you need to injure someone, do it in such a way that you do not have to fear their vengeance.

Niccolò Machiavelli

From well before 2022 continuing through the course of the war, NATO nations supplied weapons, C6ISR information, mercenaries and advisors. Contractors from these nations also worked in Ukraine who were clandestinely still under control of these NATO nations. As none of these NATO nations were in a declared state of war against the Russian Federation the legality of their actions was questionable. From top to bottom, all who were part of this needed to be brought before the law at conflict termination.

From a neocon hegemonic perspective, the US corporate state including large agribusiness was attracted by the abundant resources and fields in Crimea, Donetsk and Luhansk. From a NATO perspective the ultimate prize was Crimea and the port of Sevastopol to enable NATO control of the Black Sea, its trade routes and the resources of the area. The Russian Federation's intervention in February 2022 in Ukraine, which was essentially a civil war, involved nearly all NATO nations as co-belligerents in support of Ukraine.

For the NATO alliance there were differing reasons as to why each state gambled on trying to break up the Russian Federation to open it up for Western corporate ransacking. For the European NATO states, it made absolutely no sense. If they had worked cooperatively with Russia and unified the entire European continent, then Europe would have become the world's dominant economic power.

Do I not destroy my enemies when I make them my friends?
Abraham Lincoln

Russia was the primary reason that European industry could thrive due to competitive prices on a range of commodities. From any given political perspective there was no logical reason, to take by theft and violence, things that were readily available by cooperation and dialogue. The European Commission, EU Parliament and most EU states had gone all in, unaware that poker is not a team game.

Always assume incompetence before looking for conspiracy.
Niccolò Machiavelli

NATO had used Ukraine as a proxy to be sacrificed and carved up like a plump turkey afterwards. It had never occurred to the Europeans that the US was using Europe as a proxy to be sacrificed and was looking to carve up three turkeys. For the US, the destruction of the European economy was a nice consolation prize and very much in line with the PNAC which was about US hegemony.

The neocon project produced a massive conga line of vicious cowards and fools to support the PNAC. The Five Eyes (FVEY) Anglo collaborators were something to be expected but the number of European neocon quislings was surprising.3 These quislings were kept hidden behind the illusion of an independent Europe, exemplified by the German government when led by Angela Merkel.

3. The Five Eyes (FVEY) is an intelligence community comprising Australia, Canada, New Zealand, the United Kingdom and the United States of America.

During the Cold War a modus vivendi was still possible due to a bipolar world. The paradigm created in the wake of the cynical and deceptive Minsk II diplomacy employed by the US, NATO members and Ukraine meant that the destruction of the military was no longer sufficient to win a war.

Neocon practitioners and their belief that they were somehow exceptional became the centre of gravity. Neocon ideology was not at all a popular idea, even in the West. The global majority had already suffered tremendously under imperialism and colonialism. This latest iteration with its forever wars was even more destructive and not limited to the populace of the Global South. This ideology sought to return its own people back to serfdom.

The opportunity of defeating the enemy is provided by the enemy himself.

Sun Tzu

Machiavelli was born into the Renaissance; von Clausewitz was a child of the Enlightenment. As such, the combination of complex sciences, including nuclear arsenals and other weapons of mass destruction under the control of troglodytes did not enter their cognitive processes.

War is an extension of politics by other means. War by its very nature is always a gamble therefore it should only be used as a very last resort. Von Clausewitz, Machiavelli and Sun Tzu could not have imagined a class of politicians so reckless. This class of politician did not serve the state or its people. They were instead subordinated to ideologies and various corporate entities.

Those corporate entities had competing interests. Corporate interests were global in nature, without defined boundaries; that represented a chaotic system. It was termed 'disaster capitalism', seeking opportunities in disasters. This was the basis of privatising profits and socialising debt. The public would pay for military operations and the corporate state would benefit from cheap commodities, reconstruction or providing supplies to the MIC.

The corporate state wanted everything but corporate entities did not have the means to accomplish that task. To assist these chaotic ventures, numerous think tanks were established including The Brookings Institution, ASPI, ISW, IISS, RUSI, CFR and the RAND Corporation. These think tanks would develop plans and theories for destabilising and carving up nations, thinly disguised as defence policies or global engagement. Organisations such as the National Endowment for Democracy (NED) and a plethora of non-government organisations (NGOs) could then provide assistance in operations through their global footprint. This all-required government involvement and military assistance.

Georgia a geo-strategically significant country that borders the Russian Federation was a perfect example of NGO footprints. As of 2024 Georgia housed approximately 24,000 NGOs most of whom had international donors. The intention of these international NGOs and their funding sources were largely unknown. This is a perfect example of providing tools to create Colour Revolutions.

In the days of empire there was a grand plan for each empire defined by boundaries, therefore strategic planning was relatively straightforward. In this new paradigm there were a lot of chaotic parts that were not all rowing in the same direction. The biggest problem was the inability to understand grand strategy and its moving parts, including how both the Technological and Industrial Revolutions would affect the economics of production, logistics and the supply chain.

As part of the MIIMAC, retired generals and other high-ranking officers would regularly appear in various media, writing or speaking on strategy, tactics and military equipment. It was readily apparent as to how clueless these people were in regards to production, logistics and the supply chain. Intelligence experts were presented who could not even speak the language of their country of expertise. How could they possibly understand the culture and everything that flowed from that?

The much greater problem of a Western kakistocracy was human ego, where they attributed their own criminality to others. The US, UK and Australia created the AUKUS alliance positing that China was interested in global domination including the invasion of Australia. The body politic and NATO militaries in the US, UK and Europe screamed hysterically that the Russian Federation was interested in invading Europe. These suppositions completely disregarded massive glaring facts that only imbeciles could ignore.

Von Clausewitz mused that war was politics by other means and used the analogy of comparing war to commerce. Although this is essentially correct, these concepts apply to those who are the rulers and servants of their nation state. The corporate world in the US, UK and Europe, represented by their governments, coveted all the resources available in Belarus, Ukraine and the Russian Federation and even drew maps as to how the Russian Federation would be carved up. These governments primarily served the corporate world.

For US, UK and European states it meant that they wanted to return to a type of neo-colonialism on behalf of the corporate state, taking commodities by violent means. Commodities that were readily available to them through commerce and came at reasonable cost allowing their industries to thrive.

Had they been successful in this venture, as was proven in Ukraine, the Western corporate takeover of resources would not provide lower prices for the populace, only larger corporate profits and lower-quality goods as was the case with GM and GMO foods.

The thought that corporate theft with extreme violence was an acceptable concept in the West was thus attributed to China and the Russian Federation. Even if this concept was correct, it should have occurred to them that Europe had nothing worth stealing as they were bereft of all the things they wanted from Belarus, Ukraine and the

Russian Federation. For Russia this fight was existential, for NATO it was a corporate venture.

In 2024, the population of the European NATO countries was well over 500 million, with NATO North America representing another 380 million for a total of 880 million. The population of the Russian Federation was just under 145 million. NATO outnumbered the Russian Federation by 6 to 1.

Even if the Russian Federation wanted to be the master of Europe, basic logistical considerations meant that, it was just not feasible. In 2024 it would have required at least tripling the size of their army with accompanying air assets and a massive logistical chain in tow. It would also first require breaking NATO on the battlefield.

The Soviet Union was able to defeat the Nazis during World War II by halting their advance at the gates of Moscow (autumn 1941), attritting them in Stalingrad and other places (autumn and winter 1942–43) and finally by breaking them in Kursk (summer 1943). Once this was accomplished, they had sufficient forces and material to drive the Nazis all the way back to Berlin before commencing the final assault. These were the hammer blows absorbing, attritting and defeating Blitzkrieg.

In 2023 the Russian Federation had halted a counteroffensive with in-depth defensive lines in Donetsk and Luhansk. They then attritted a NATO proxy army in Ukraine waiting to see if NATO was dumb enough to repeat history.

As of 2024 China could produce just about anything made in the West at lower cost due to many factors. In terms of technology China was ahead of the West in most areas. Sanctions placed on the Russian Federation by the West allowed China to acquire most necessary commodities at a reasonable price. By means of skilful commerce, China had become the greatest industrial power in the history of the world.

If the West had spent more on education rather than military junk and adventurism, they may have realised that being the greatest industrial nation in the emerging Technological Revolution had certain disadvantages and could therefore work that to their own advantage. They were instead clueless as to how the Technological Revolution would develop.

Allowing the Industrial Revolution to be shaped in a laissez-faire manner had brought humanity to edge of the abyss in about 200 years; the Technological Revolution left to develop on its own could finish the job in 20 years.

The Communist Party of China (CPC) was run by largely pragmatic politicians educated in science, technology, engineering and mathematics (STEM). In China the State controlled capital. The financial reality of stealing resources through means of violence would increase costs at least 10-fold therefore not something logical people would consider.

In regards to the Australia, United Kingdom, United States (AUKUS) alliance, the US perspective was about further fattening their MIC, protecting their surveillance and intelligence gathering assets in Australia and using the country for operating bases. For the UK this was about the UK MIC and military contracts. In Australia this was paranoia formed from a childlike fear of the bogeyman coming in the night.

Australia had no credible plan for militarily defending its borders on its own. Its defence acquisitions were based on being an adjunct to the US military. As such they signed onto a 'strategy' that thought confronting China in the Strait of Malacca and the South China Sea might be a good idea. The very areas where China was strongest and had prepared in-depth defences.

In 2024 China did not possess a navy capable of in-depth operations. In the 21st century, in-depth naval operations were no longer feasible due to modern weapons systems and the lethality of submarines and UUVs. To run a naval gauntlet from China to Australia would be unaffordable in terms of material losses.

If you were to attempt to invade a country with geo-strategic depth such as Australia, taking a city like Darwin would require assembling the largest seaborne invasion force and the greatest logistical supply chain in the history of the world. It would dwarf the Normandy landings conducted in World War II and would come at a tremendous financial cost in addition to human lives just to establish a foothold. To what end?

In any war involving China and the US, there were several FVEY surveillance bases in Australia that would need to be destroyed by the People's Liberation Army (PLA). This task could be accomplished easily with precision guided missiles.

China's PLA possessed a nuclear triad but constrained itself with a no nuclear first strike policy. As such, this policy included a no nuclear strike against any nation that did not possess nuclear weapons. As of 2023 the Australian government abandoned that protection by allowing nuclear armed B-52 bombers to operate from the Tindall Airbase in the Northern Territory. Australia had also signed preliminary agreements to purchase nuclear-powered submarines that used highly enriched uranium (HEU).

The F-35s that Australia already possessed and the nuclear-powered submarines they wished to acquire were both capable of delivering nuclear weapon payloads. There was of course no way of distinguishing between an Australian F-35 or a US F-35 operating on Australian soil.

From 2023, in case of war, a B-52 starting its engines would have to be considered a nuclear first strike action in progress and an F-35 taking off could be considered in the same light. China possessed nuclear capable hypersonic missiles that could reach Northern Australia within 20 minutes.

The West's primary tool of persuasion had been destroyed in NATO's war on the Russian Federation. The sanctions placed on the Russian Federation was the final nail in the West's coffin. To deprive yourself of commodities from one of the largest producers in the world, thereby increasing your own costs and inflation, was an historical act of stupidity.

There are very few men–and they are the exceptions–who are able to think and feel beyond the present moment.

Carl von Clausewitz

The West's and in particular the US's great advantage was the US dollar (USD) as the world's reserve currency, because this fiat currency was used globally for trading oil and gas. Trading oil and gas in USD created an artificial demand that enabled the unfettered printing of USD creating tremendous debt without resultant hyperinflation.

The result of these sanctions was the rest of the world no longer solely trading oil and gas in USD. This exposed a heavily indebted US to hyperinflation. It set in motion a game of reducing a nation's USD exposure without acting too aggressively lest the value was to drop too quickly whilst still holding significant stock.

The US government had racked up the greatest debt in human history. As of early 2024 that federal debt exceeded 123 percent of Gross Domestic Product (GDP). Annual federal spending was 1.3 times the total tax revenue. Total US unfunded liabilities were 7.64 times GDP which was approximately 28 trillion USD at the time.

In the West the body politic was working directly against the interest of its own people at the expense of the taxpayer. They were largely responsible for the slaughter in Ukraine and remained shamefully silent about the slaughter in Gaza.

The Europeans had been attacked by their ally, destroying Nordstream pipelines, a critical piece of infrastructure. Pretending not to know who attacked them displayed a cowardice unparalleled in Europe's history. It was also an act of treachery against their own people. The West had set itself on a course of suicide, unable to comprehend entrenched barriers of dogma, arrogance, and insecurities instead believing their own narratives.

Destroying the enemy required accurately identifying the 'head' and all of its support structure including 'allies'. That structure was composed mostly of civilians. These 'civilians' were in fact the main belligerents. In this ideology 'exceptional' people do not do their own killing and dying, they left that to proxies or their serfs.

The legal definition of legitimate wartime targets needed to be expanded. The termination of conflict and the path to peace could only be enabled by prosecuting all those responsible, providing justice and therefore healing to the injured.

It is always preferential that the enemy's judiciary deals with their own war criminals to provide agency for their own people. Unfortunately, we must again adhere to von Clausewitz's doctrines in order for justice to be delivered. The complete annihilation of a military that stands in the way of justice must be regarded as the prime objective of all engagements.

In this new paradigm, any action had to address the problem from root to stem. An ideology so degenerate, that it sets itself against humanity and nature, had to be decapitated before any healing process could begin.

CHAPTER 9

ATHENA'S GRACE

The gravity of the political, social and economic situation in the 21st century demanded fundamental changes to economic systems, including abolition of perpetual economic growth, properly pricing externalities, strict regulation of markets and property acquisition and reigning in corporate lobbying. It required an honest media and judiciary committed to truth, justice and equality. Above all it required a complete reformation of the education system.

A sign of intelligence is an awareness of one's own ignorance.
Niccolò Machiavelli

When a human baby is born it is entirely helpless; others have to feed it, change it, bathe it etc. This develops a very normal expectation that everything will be taken care of. We all start at the centre of our own universe. A healthy human child with parental guidance develops perspective, shifting the focus on self to self-and-others as the brain matures.

Western culture, particularly Anglo culture was focussed on the individual; the self. The neocon generation was conceived in this culture and came predominately from well-to-do families. This combination was not ideal for the development of empathy, keeping the self very much at the centre of development. Narcissism and elements of psychopathy thrive in this type of environment.

As higher education became increasingly commercialised in the West, standards started to decrease. Critical thinking skills were very much disregarded in this period, replaced with ideological absolutes. China, Russia and Iran vastly outstripped the West in STEM graduates.

Neocons were formed from a mal-educated, privileged elite that had not developed emotionally. They believed themselves to be exceptional and that led to where it always leads. Human lives were something to be toyed with by overgrown children, who would throw a tantrum if things did not go as planned.

By the delusions of seeming good the people are often misled to desire their own ruin; and they are frequently influenced by great hopes and brave promises.

Niccolò Machiavelli

Human ego provides a lens through which people see themselves. If something is good for me then it will also benefit the majority; somehow. Neocons; US President Joe Biden, heckled as 'Genocide Joe' by protesters and EU Commission President Ursula von der Leyen, referred to as 'Frau Genocide' in the EU Parliament, saw themselves as benevolent. When looking at the actions carried out and listening to various speeches, the monikers became obvious.

Because there is no man who can be a true and just judge of himself, so much will self-love deceive him.

Dante Alighieri

Neocon ideology as the new centre of gravity could only be overcome by bringing its advocates to justice and preventing its return by superior ideas. Considering that this ideology was not at all popular, it should have been easy to overcome.

The preferred strategy is to break the enemy's resistance without fighting and that requires superior ideas. Superior ideas need to be enduring and that requires ongoing human consensus. To this end, a society that others wish to emulate must be created.

It is easy to love your friend, but sometimes the hardest lesson to learn is to love your enemy.

Sun Tzu

Autarky, otherwise known as self-sufficiency is key to maintaining societal harmony and is crucial in winning any military engagement. All States must have sufficient housing, food, water and energy for the populace during peace, winter and war. Self-sufficiency is a cornerstone of security.

Autarky is a concept that must be applied from bottom to top; it applies from the individual up to the state level and beyond and provides independence. The most significant benefit of autarky is the destratification of society.

Independence comes from financial freedom; it provides choice and security. The individuality that independence brings is important, not as a justification for selfishness but as a way to generate new ideas and original thinking. A society cannot allow itself to fall into the groupthink that has so far driven humanity's violent history.

Only a fool learns from his own mistakes. The wise man learns from the mistakes of others.

Otto von Bismarck

Emotional intelligence and its core component, empathy, is the key to the avoidance of war. Narcissistic economic ideology develops low emotional intelligence. Co-operative economic systems are dependent on advanced emotional intelligence.

Economic activity must find its balance in nature. The prime lesson of the Industrial Revolution is that it is not possible to subordinate nature to human economics without tremendous self-harm.

A return to first principles in a republic is sometimes caused by the simple virtues of one man. His good example has such an influence that the good men strive to imitate him, and the wicked are ashamed to lead a life so contrary to his example.

Niccolò Machiavelli

The education system needs a complete overhaul with autarky as the starting point. A society had been developed that has no means of self-reliance. If supermarkets ran out of food the masses would starve. Life sciences such as learning how to grow fruits and vegetables need to be incorporated into education.

Consider your origins: you were not made to live as brutes, but to follow virtue and knowledge.

Dante Alighieri

Social sciences regarding human development need to be taught in order to understand the needs of children growing into adulthood. Raising and socialising children should not be unknown to the parents of a new-born. A healthy society can only be derived from functional families that have emotional intelligence.

A meritocracy is empirically driven and is the cornerstone of advanced societies. It should never be who you know that brings advancement. In this regard, all private schools need to be abolished. In the West, STEM subjects need far more attention in all levels of education.

Talent and genius operate outside the rules, and theory conflicts with practice.

Carl von Clausewitz

Education must include the socialisation of students and that means working together; the strong helping the weak. It means learning about all religions and atheism in order to foster understanding across all cultures. It means casting aside any sense of exceptionalism. Critical thinking requires an accurate understanding of history and its perspectives.

At the tertiary level, education should provide for workplace integration in addition to purely theoretical science, technology, engineering, arts and mathematics (STEAM) for the gifted.

Be convinced that to be happy means to be free and that to be free means to be brave, therefore do not take lightly the perils of war.

Thucydides

Considering the capabilities of modern nuclear and biological weapons humanity's future ends in one of two ways; extinction of our species or in a co-operative manner of managing our collective destiny. Athena offers us the defeat and banishment of Ares; all that is required is honour, moral courage and empathy. The stars await us.

www.ingramcontent.com/pod-product-compliance
Lightning Source LLC
Chambersburg PA
CBHW050538280326
41933CB00011B/1639